D0835935

Chesapeake Bay

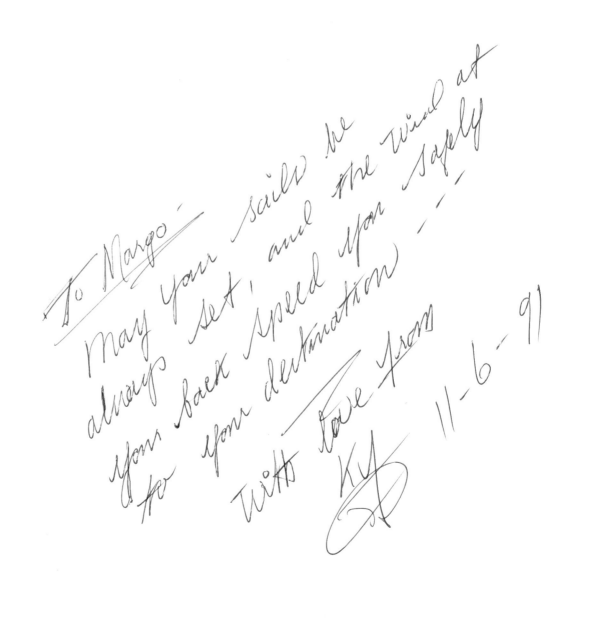

To Margo -
May your sails be
always set, and the wind at
your back speed you safely
to your destination —

With love from
KY
11-6-91

Chesapeake Bay

Photographs by Robert Grieser.

Captions by Robert Grieser and Peter P. Baker, *The Baltimore Sun*

Introduction by James A. Michener

Harry N. Abrams, Inc., Publishers, New York

To my father, Robert H. Grieser, Sr.,
A loving memory

Editor: Robert Morton
Designer: Bob McKee

LIBRARY OF CONGRESS CATALOGING-IN-PUBLICATION DATA
Grieser, Robert, 1946–
Chesapeake Bay: photographs / by Robert Grieser;
introduction by James A. Michener.
p.   cm.   ISBN 0–8109–3159–1
1. Chesapeake Bay (Md. and Va.)—Description and
travel—Views. 2. Chesapeake Bay Region (Md. and Va.)—
Description and travel—Views.   I. Title.
F187.C5G75   1990
975.5'18043'0222—dc20   89–38992
CIP

Photographs copyright © 1990 Robert Grieser
Introduction copyright © 1990 James A. Michener
Published in 1990 by Harry N. Abrams, Incorporated, New
York. All rights reserved. No part of the contents of this
book may be reproduced without the written permission of
the publisher. A Times Mirror Company
Printed and bound in Japan

TITLE PAGE:
Fireworks burst over the dome of the state capitol in
Annapolis, Maryland, during the bicentennial celebration in
1976. This burst was unauthorized—the official fireworks
were set off a mile away at the United States Naval Academy
on the banks of the Severn River. From November 1783
to August 1784, Annapolis was the capital of the
United States.

Contents

During the years I lived along the Chesapeake Bay, working on my novel dealing with that splendid body of water, I became aware of the excellent photographic work being done by Bob Grieser. He worked for a Washington newspaper and was quite good at catching the faces of people in the news, in depicting action in a typical story, and in adjusting his skills to just about anything that came along. In other words, he was a solid craftsman who knew what he was doing.

I met many such men, and several women. What made Grieser special, particularly for me, was his avocation. Whenever he found time he was on the Chesapeake, photographing its many moods. He sailed with professionals to record their experiences; he roamed the shores to watch the action of the waves; he perched himself in unusual spots to catch varied aspects of life along the reaches of the bay; and what impressed me most, he bought himself a small boat so that he could go out upon the water to photograph ships and boats of all kinds as they sailed past.

I had several occasions to see Grieser's work, and always I learned something new from what he had been doing. I liked the catholicity of his taste, for invariably he produced pictures that covered new aspects of the bay's appearance. He was good at depicting storms, the passage of wild life, the varied types of boats that sailed the bay, the people who frequented it at work and those at play.

In time I realized that Bob had taken upon himself the job of compiling a complete record of the bay as it existed in the late 1970s. He intended to present a visual record of the enormous richness of this excellent inland sea, and the more I saw of his compilation the more I applauded what he was up to.

In the end he would have a fascinating selection of photographs, varied in style, rich in texture and highly personal. This would be the bay that I had been trying to describe, and a great deal more.

For example, I had focused on the wildlife, the storms, the ice-bound waters, the various craft that plied the bay commercially, the shipbuilding, the recreational use. Bob had stunning pictures of all these aspects, and his photographs usually showed a little more detail than I had gone into.

I had decided early in my own work *not* to deal with other aspects of the bay which were equally important, but which I felt were not germane to my story, and I was especially interested in what Bob achieved with these subjects, for he showed me what I might have accomplished had I pursued those additional story lines.

He had some great shots of Smith Island and Tangier Island, those extraordinary enclaves in the bay where history stands still. I remember talking with a young woman from Tangier one day: she, her husband, all her family and all his family had the same family name. "And we have had, for many generations." A writer would like to explore that astonishing statement, but I felt that these islands could better be dealt with by some other writer. Grieser gives a good pictorial account of them.

Every time I saw one of the remarkable bay lighthouses I wanted to include a representative one in my novel; there was no logical place to do so. Bob has given us a choice group of shots catching the romance and solitude of these structures.

I did a lot of riding on ferries when I was doing my research but was able to utilize the material only briefly. Bob has improved on that.

I decided early in the working out of my novel that the city of Baltimore was too big a subject for me to tackle adequately, especially its magnificent inner harbor, so I was glad to see what Bob was able to accomplish with this, and the *Constellation* and the *Pride of Baltimore,* which then resided there with such distinction.

In my worksheets for the novel I had many pages dealing with log canoes, one of the world's most fascinating and insane crafts. I was captivated by them and had planned to use a log canoe race as a main feature of my final chapter, even interrogating crews and learning some of the magic that keeps the little boats afloat. But when it came time to writing about them, the story had drifted off in other directions, so my work came to naught. Grieser has caught these strange things to perfection: these frail, narrow canoes with no keel and idiotic height and sweep of sail. To anyone who knows boats it is quite obvious they cannot stay afloat, but they do, as Bob's pictures show.

On one aspect of the bay Bob and I agree. It is a most fickle and dangerous body of water. In the relatively brief time that I worked upon it, sailing in all types of craft, venturing upon it in all kinds of weather, twenty-one professional watermen lost their lives during sudden storms, or in gales of unexpected fury. Huge boats were capsized; others were turned end over end; the safest craft on the bay were suddenly engulfed; men who had known the water all their lives reached once too often for a rope and were lost.

I have never known another body of water so placid on a good day, or so easy to navigate in a mild storm. Since there are no rocky shores, one simply drives his boat inland, leaves it to the waves and walks ashore. Many have saved their lives in this way, for the shores are not inhospitable the way they are in rock-bound Maine. A child could sail this bay, and many do.

But when clouds gather in the southwest and begin to roar northward, watch out. I have never known another body of water whose surface could change with such violent rapidity. I have been caught this way three times, and it scared the devil out of me.

Bob's pictures of small craft in heavy seas are some of the choice shots in this book. They remind me of what the bay can be.

James A. Michener

The Land and Shore

It is, by most accounts, a gentle land where winter is harsh but
seldom and the other seasons tick by in largely pleasing
fashion. It is a land that tumbles down slowly from the
mountains of Pennsylvania, the Virginias, and Western
Maryland to the shores of rivers great and small, toward the
intriguing expanse of Chesapeake Bay, and then toward a large
peninsula known as the Eastern Shore.

It is a land mostly fostered by the Chesapeake, from the
plantation docks along its rivers, creeks, and inlets, where
planters shipped tobacco east to Europe and brought people,
stuffs, and lifestyles west to the colonies. The land has been
settled through almost four centuries of evolution and by the
resolution of battles and issues great and small—from the
conflicts of the Revolution and the Civil War to the riots for
civil rights.

In 1608 Captain John Smith described this land as *such
pleasant plaine, hils and fertile valleyes, and watered so conveniently
with their sweete brooks and cristall springs, as if art itselfe had
devised them.* But the land and bay are beset by acid rain and
the runoff of farm pesticides, fertilizers, and hazardous waste.
Here, marine life is hard pressed to overcome the vagaries of
men who build cities, pave roads, and build bridges—and until
recently paid little heed to a unique resource dying. Still, by
most accounts, it is a land and shore of pleasant living for
people great and small.

OPPOSITE:

Near the head of Chesapeake Bay, Concord Light stands tall at the entrance to the Susquehanna River and the narrow, dredged channel to City Park in the town of Havre de Grace, Maryland. The Chesapeake Bay covers the river bed of the old Susquehanna, flooded out when the last Ice Age receded.

OVERLEAF:

Now fully automated, but still the site of a U.S. Coast Guard station, Cove Point Light provides a backdrop for visitors as they stroll on the beach.

At Thomas Point, the original lighthouse (built in 1825) stood on land. In 1874, that structure was replaced by a "screwpile" lighthouse a half-mile off Thomas Point Shoal. The light's 6,000-candlepower beacon, shining through a fresnel lens fabricated in Paris, can be seen for 12 miles. Thomas Point Light, the last manned lighthouse on Chesapeake Bay until it was automated in 1986, is listed in the National Register of Historic Places.

Ice damage from the winter of 1976–77 has caused Sharps Island Light to list slightly to port. Located just south of Tilghman Island on Maryland's Eastern Shore, Sharps Island Light marks the entrance to the Choptank River and some of the best fishing, crabbing, and oystering in the Chesapeake estuary.

OPPOSITE:

Just north of the Bay Bridges, Sandy Point Light marks a shoal along the Chesapeake's Western Shore a short distance south of the entrance to Craighill Channel and Baltimore, an international port of entry. The lighthouse has been boarded up to prevent vandalism.

The largest known specimen of white oak and Maryland's official state tree is the 450-year-old Wye Oak, which stands in Wye Oak State Park, the state's smallest. The park is between Centreville and Easton on the Eastern Shore.

OVERLEAF:

A bicyclist traverses a field near Port Royal, Virginia, as the sun's rays peak from behind a thunderhead in the west. Squall lines rumble eastward often during the summer months, when moisture from the southeast is trapped against the Blue Ridge Mountains to the west and circulated by westerly winds east toward the Bay.

OPPOSITE TOP:

Overlooking the Rhode and West rivers on
Maryland's Western Shore is Java Farm, whose
manor house was built in the mid-1800s and
burned about the turn of the century. The black
walnuts surrounding the ruin are believed to
comprise the largest black walnut orchard in
the state.

OPPOSITE BOTTOM:

Typical of Victorian architecture throughout the
Chesapeake region, the Villa de Sales, built in
1884, is a reminder of a bygone era—when
gingerbread eaves and hand-worked railings were
the pride of craftsmen, and wide, wraparound
porches provided shade or shelter and a place to
catch the evening breeze.

OVERLEAF:

A fresh snowfall puts a white bloom on the fields
of winter and a barn long in disrepair in Calvert
County.

OPPOSITE TOP:

Early in this century, this tractor ran rough over the farm fields of its owner. Now, bramble creeps over its empty seat and silent treads.

OPPOSITE BOTTOM:

In St. Mary's County, in southern Maryland, the pace is a little slower and for some—like this farmer working a team of horses in front of a tobacco barn—life's values are carefully weighed and, perhaps, the paths more carefully chosen.

OVERLEAF:

Working a field the modern way, a farmer near Salisbury on Maryland's lower Eastern Shore discs as the sun sinks low.

Children share a pony ride in a rural setting south
of Annapolis in Anne Arundel County.

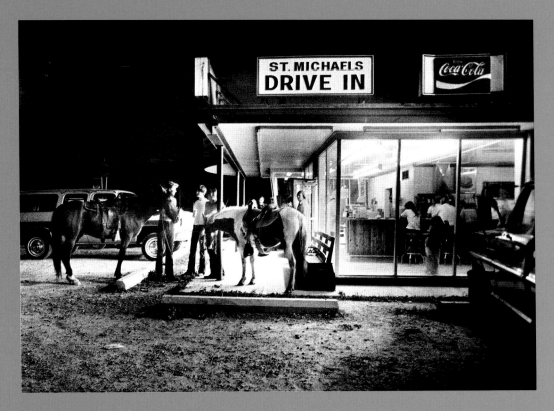

Drive in or ride in, it doesn't matter at the St.
Michael's Drive In, where people gather for a
burger, fries, and something cold to drink.

Lorea's Tavern in Annapolis was a favorite spot
for watermen and politicians, lawyers, and stone
masons. As late as 1974, a can of beer cost but 15
cents and a straight pour of whiskey was little
more. Mary, the crab lady, would drop by to sell
homemade crab cakes between crackers for
a quarter.

OPPOSITE:
Two tugs make their way south on the Chesapeake with an uncommonly heavy tow of grain barges. The lead tug provides the main pulling power; the other helps with steerage. In the past, commercial traffic was heavy on the Chesapeake and the two-score rivers that flow into it directly. Since the building of the Bay Bridges near Annapolis and the Chesapeake Bay Bridge-Tunnel at the mouth of the Bay, much of the commercial traffic is now on the state roads and superhighways.

Seagulls now are the only crew aboard an old, shallow-draft crab boat tied in a creek off the Hampton River near the commercial fishing docks in Hampton, Virginia.

A privately owned ferry, the *Southside*, crosses the Tred Avon River on Maryland's Eastern Shore. The ferry service between the towns of Oxford and Bellevue runs from sunrise to sundown with extended hours in the summer.

OVERLEAF:
As sunrise lights Annapolis Harbor, a pair of locals try netting blue crabs from the docks at the Hilton Hotel. The blue crab is plentiful and popular among fishermen and diners along Chesapeake Bay.

An old house is moved by barge along the
Patuxent River from Benedict to Lower Marlboro.

OPPOSITE:

Pushed ashore by a December storm, *Water Lily*
lies on the rocks along the shore of Herring Bay.
Bruce Alexander Bodine, a young bay pilot and
former tugboat skipper, spent several months
working on *Water Lily* while preparing to refloat
her in deeper water.

OVERLEAF:

Tied to a post and apparently forgotten, a small
skiff weathers in the sun at Lake Ogleton off the
Severn River near Annapolis.

ABOVE:

Potential buyers look over *Betty R*, an old, 36-foot Chesapeake deadrise workboat. On the shore at Kent Narrows, the boat has been out of the water awhile and is dry and opening at the seams.

LEFT:

Mud dries in the shallow flats of the South River, leaving a group of older wooden boats high and dry. Since the advent of fiberglass as the primary building material for pleasure boats, graveyards for wooden boats are becoming more commonplace. Eventually, salvors will haul the hulks to a spot and burn them, later reclaiming the scrap metal from their fastenings and fittings.

OPPOSITE:

When winds on the Chesapeake blow strong out of the northwest for a day or two, the water gets even thinner in back bays and coves like this one in Galesville, Maryland.

OPPOSITE TOP:

The hazy, lazy days of summer find a young reader floating on a raft in Church Creek off the South River below Annapolis.

OPPOSITE BOTTOM:

The headwaters of some rivers that feed the Chesapeake provide another watersport; this kayaker paddles his way through a whitewater course on the Potomac River above Harpers Ferry, West Virginia.

OVERLEAF:

A water-skier slaloms back across the wake of his tow boat, throwing up a wall of spray that seems to hang in the early light near Round Bay on the Severn River above Annapolis.

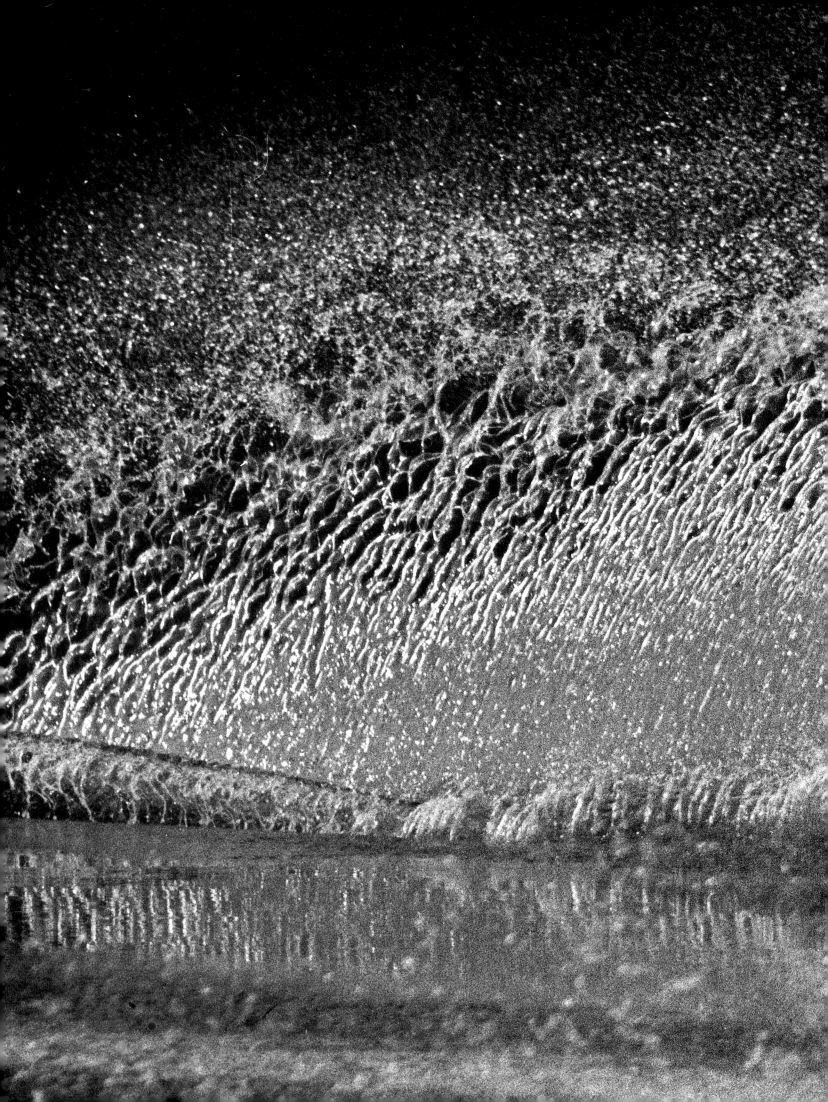

Reflected in the still water of one of the many small ponds scattered through the Delaware–Maryland–Virginia peninsula, an angler awaits the strike of a big bass near Salisbury, Maryland.

A remote control sailboat appears to be chasing a duck as it heads for its racing mark. Model boat racing can be found at various cities around the Chesapeake Bay.

OPPOSITE BOTTOM:

With its wings set for braking, a mallard duck comes in for a landing on a sun-glistening creek near the Sassafras River on Maryland's upper Eastern Shore.

OVERLEAF:

An immature gull, its feathers not yet fully white, soars above a creek off the Elk River, its neck craned while keeping a watchful eye for something to eat.

As the sun peeks over the treetops on Maryland's Eastern Shore, hundreds of Canada geese return to a pond at Wye Mills.

OVERLEAF:

A flock of Canada geese takes flight with a thunderous drumming of wings as an intruder approaches near Cambridge, Maryland. The Delmarva Peninsula is a major stopping place along the Eastern Flyway for these visitors from the north.

An adult osprey (right) and a fledgling share a
nest at the entrance to Lake Ogleton off the
Severn River. Adolescent birds have mottled
feathers on heads and wings, while the adults have
solid color feathers with white head feathers
and a pronounced dark streak on either side
of the head.

OPPOSITE:

A great blue heron stands motionless in the
marshy headwaters of Herring Bay near Deal on
the Western Shore of the Chesapeake.

ABOVE:

Returning to the nest with a fish in its talons, an adult osprey comes in for a landing. Its wings set back and feathers down, it stalls and drops into the nest.

RIGHT:

A mother osprey, with a fish held tightly in her talons, returns to the nest. Known as the fish hawk, the osprey is a fearsome hunter, soaring 50 feet above the water and then diving for the surface like a stone. Just before hitting the water, the hawk extends its powerful talons and with a splash—and some luck—lands its prey; menhaden, eel, or catfish.

OPPOSITE:

An intruder approaching a feeding roost causes an osprey to lift off, carrying an eel.

ABOVE:

A great horned owl waits patiently for the perfect moment to swoop down on its prey.

OPPOSITE:

This great horned owl looks ready to attack. Owls are common throughout the Delmarva Peninsula, but are rarely seen because they are nocturnal hunters.

OVERLEAF:

Birdhouses for purple martins dot the shoreline of a marsh near the head of Hunting Creek off the Choptank River. Martins help control flies and mosquitoes during the summer months. This bird village is near Preston, Maryland.

ABOVE:

A trio of mallards seems to pause to take in a sign posted at the end of a dock in Georgetown, Maryland, on the Sassafras River.

OPPOSITE TOP:

With the late afternoon sun casting shadows, a man and his dog walk among the broken ice along the shore of the frozen Potomac River in Washington, D.C.

OPPOSITE BOTTOM:

A good samaritan feeds waterfowl from the end of the city docks in Annapolis. During the winter, shallow creeks and marshes freeze, forcing the birds to look elsewhere for open water and food.

ABOVE:

A dock damaged by ice and a small sailboat frozen in place at Harness Creek off the South River are reminders of winter's fury during the big freeze of 1976–77.

OPPOSITE:

In the icy waters of Chesapeake Beach, a pram lies highlighted by the winter sun.

OVERLEAF:

The tidal rise and fall of the Potomac in winter leaves chunks of ice covering a walkway in East Potomac Park in Washington, D.C.

At least once a year in the towns along Chesapeake Bay a good snowstorm keeps children out of school and parents out of the office—and gives good neighbors the opportunity to help a motorist down a snowy street in Annapolis.

OVERLEAF:

During the big freeze of 1976–77, people walked on the Potomac River, but Eastern Shore folk proved even more daring, strolling several hundred yards from shore. This view is looking west from the shore end of the Bay Bridges. The ice ranged from 18 to 24 inches thick, but officials advised people to stay off the ice because of weak spots. The last time the Bay froze this deeply was in the late 1930s.

OPPOSITE AND ABOVE:

On the last leg of a paint job that takes eight years to complete, young workers sandblast, chip, scrape, and paint the Chesapeake Bay Bridges—and about the time the job is finished, it must be started all over again. More than 100 gallons of paint or primer are sprayed and brushed on the steel structures every day. Workers toil each day except Sunday from spring to fall when the weather is good and the winds are below 22 knots. Some banana oil is mixed with the aluminum paint to make it shine.

OVERLEAF:

Built some twenty years apart, the Chesapeake Bay Bridges join the western and eastern shores of Maryland. The older bridge was completed in 1952 and is 4.4 miles from shore to shore, exclusive of entry ramps. The towers of its center span are 348 feet above the Bay.

Watermen and Others

Between the raging surf of the Atlantic Ocean and the
soft lap of the tides of Chesapeake Bay lies a peninsula
encompassing the tiny state of Delaware, a fair portion of
Maryland, and a long spit of land belonging to Virginia.

It is known overall as Delmarva. Its largest part is known to
Marylanders as the Eastern Shore, a land of rivers broad and
narrow, deep and shallow, of creeks that wind for miles
through marshland, and of waters so thin that great mud flats
are exposed at low tide.

From these creeks, the watermen come with each faint
dawn—some beneath a cloud of stained sail aboard the
venerable skipjacks of America's last commercial sailing fleet,
others within the rumble of engines aboard wooden workboats
that chip and leak and peel progressively as the seasons
move on.

They come for crabs or fish in the warm-weather months,
for oysters in winter, when ice often is on the rigging. It is not
a life for fair-weather men.

Indeed, these men play to their own tune—the drumming
of a tow line as a mis-set dredge beats in the deep across an
oyster bar; the rhythm of a hand-tonger's feet on wooden
washboards as a deadrise workboat lifts and falls on a benign
Chesapeake.

ABOVE:

Often at odds with each other are those who
work the Bay and those who play on it. Here,
Compromise sails close by *Lady Ruth IV,* whose
crew is harvesting oysters.

OPPOSITE TOP:

On a shimmering section of Eastern Bay, a solitary
hand-tonger works a section of oysterbed. Hand-
tongs are 16- to 20-foot shafts of ash attached to
curved, metal-mesh scoops. By working the shafts
in tandem, a good hand-tonger can efficiently
work a bed of oysters unseen far below his boat.

OPPOSITE BOTTOM:

After a few more strikes at the "rock," as
watermen call oyster bars, this waterman will be
ready to start culling his catch.

Wade Murphy, Jr. stands at the rail of *Sigsbee*, a skipjack
he owned and skippered until 1984. Murphy said, "You
get attached to any boat you work on for nineteen years.
I made my living on her for all that time." *Sigsbee* is one
of a dwindling number of skipjacks—boats that dredge
oyster bars largely by sail power—that still work the
Chesapeake Bay.

OPPOSITE:

Sigsbee motors through the channel from the Choptank
River toward Tilghman Island. After a day of dredging,
her decks are awash with a catch of icy oysters. Oyster
season runs from October 1 to March 31.

OVERLEAF:

With a few oysters caught in his hand-tongs, a waterman
walks back toward the middle of his boat to dump the catch
on the culling board. There he will sort the oysters by
size, keeping those three inches or more in width and
immediately passing others over the side and back into
the oyster bed.

OPPOSITE:

As the early morning sun peers beneath a line of cloud, and ocean-going ships await their turns at the docks in Baltimore, a pair of crabbers check their pots off Tolly Point at the mouth of the Severn River. Crabbing is a major source of warm-weather income for watermen and a source of recreational fishing for sportsmen young and old.

RIGHT:

Crew members aboard a skipjack haul in a dredge and dump the load on deck to be culled. Rocks and other rubbish also have to be sorted from the legal-size oysters. The crew works on a profit-sharing basis; the boat receives a share for maintenance, fuel, and food, and the remainder is usually divided equally among all crew members and the captain.

RIGHT:

A hand-tonger returns to port to sell his daily catch on Tilghman Island, a center for seafood packing and transport on Maryland's Eastern Shore. The catch is measured in bushels and each bucket is recorded for proper payment.

A pair of the famous Chesapeake Bay deadrise
workboats, rigged with hydraulic patent tongs,
work a bar off Whitehall Bay on the Western
Shore above Annapolis, trying to get a day's worth
of oysters before a storm blows in from the
southeast. In the past decade, the oyster harvest
has been diminishing at a rate that has alarmed
environmentalists and watermen alike.

Many watermen have given up their long-handled
tongs to work the bay's bottom with hydraulic
patent tong rigs, which some oystermen feel chew
up the oyster bars because of their high-powered
scissors action. Mechanized boats are not allowed
to work the same beds as hand-tongers.

He was known as Captain Earl to most of those
who met him on the waterfront along the West
River in Galesville, Maryland, where he squatted
on a piece of public waterfront and stayed for
many years. He raised an old houseboat on stilts,
drove pilings for a rickety pier, and set his
fisherman's nets down river. His surname was
Trott and his greatest enjoyments were fresh fish,
cold beer, and telling stories under the shade trees.
Capt. Earl Trott died early in the eighties; his pier
has been replaced by a small park.

Throughout the tidewater reaches of the Bay
during oyster season, shuckers, who are paid by
the bucket of oysters cleared from their shells,
exercise a dying skill.

OVERLEAF:

A champion crab-picker: Marilyn Davis has won
the title during annual competitions over the years
at the Crisfield, Maryland, Seafood Festival. Most
days during the crab season, Marilyn and her
coworkers arrive at the packing houses about
dawn and pick crabmeat until afternoon. They are
paid by the pound.

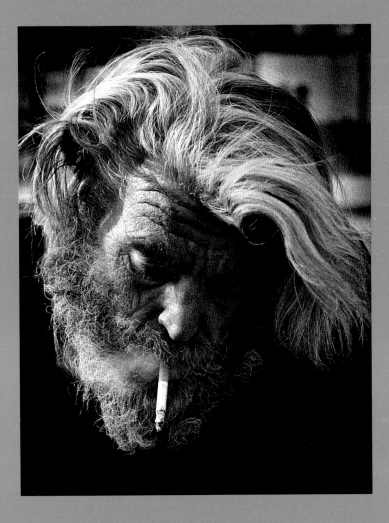

A landmark around Washington, Captain Bill
claimed he once had been in the Navy. After living
on the streets for more than 20 years, he also said
"the waterfront just isn't the same anymore since
they ruined it," meaning by its renovation.

OPPOSITE:
Once a familiar sight along the Washington, D.C.,
waterfront, this bearded fellow with blue eyes
could spin a yarn or two about the sea.

At first glance, a skipjack appears to be hard
aground on the low-tide mud flats off Rhodes
Point on Smith Island. A closer inspection reveals
that it is a model of *Lorraine Rose*, which once
sailed out of Smith Island and Crisfield.

An old deadrise workboat left to rot along the shores of
the Little Annemessex River near Crisfield, Maryland, a
reminder of the beauty and hardship of a threatened
style of life.

OVERLEAF:
There are probably more boat builders in Deltaville,
Virginia, than any other place on the Chesapeake Bay.
Both wooden and fiberglass boats are constructed
throughout the area. This 51-foot sports fisherman is
seen under construction in the shed at Miller Marine
Railway.

OPPOSITE:

The *Martha Lewis* (left) leads some of her competitors across a shimmering sea during a skipjack race held each year off Sandy Point between Baltimore and Annapolis. The next day she will don her oyster dredges to begin the working season.

ABOVE:

Chesapeake Bay skipjacks race in the northern Bay during one of several events held each year.

OVERLEAF:

Skipjacks raft together in a lagoon at Sandy Point State Park during an annual Chesapeake Appreciation Days Regatta. The regatta, held before the start of each oystering season, pays tribute to craft old and new that sail the bay to dredge for oysters.

At sunrise, skipjacks pull their dredges across the oyster beds in the Choptank River.

BELOW:

In the Choptank River, *Sigsbee,* a skipjack built in 1901 on Deal Island, pulls her dredge across an oyster bed. In 1984, *Sigsbee* was bought by *Chesapeake Bay Magazine* publisher Richard Royer and donated to the Skipjack Heritage Foundation. The purpose of the foundation is to acquire skipjacks, maintain them as working vessels and thereby prevent their ultimate disappearance from the Chesapeake Bay.

OVERLEAF:

Blasting along on a close reach, *Geneva May* sails north of the Bay Bridges during the Appreciation Days Regatta. Like many of the skipjack fleet, she has seen better days—though *Geneva May* survived a sinking at Tilghman Island in the summer of 1982. Before the turn of the last century, there were hundreds of skipjacks working the Bay; today there are fewer than thirty.

Chesapeake Log Sailing Canoes

They are, as James A. Michener says in his introduction to this book, "one of the world's most fascinating and insane crafts," these Chesapeake Bay log sailing canoes that glide along with incredible speed in fair breezes or buck and start and topple over when the wind comes up.

They are the only native American sailing craft—having evolved from the dugout canoes used by American Indians before Europeans began to settle here. Those that sail now are property and province of a small group of Eastern Shore men and women who race a circuit on the Maryland Shore from the Choptank River north to the Chester River.

And they often are a shoreman's favorite way of having fun.

The bottoms of most log canoes were built from three logs of old-growth loblolly pine, the outer faces being carefully curved and the inner faces carefully hollowed and pinned together. They are generally sprit-rigged with leg-o-mutton sails carried on two masts, with the foresail the larger. Most carry a bowsprit and a jib—and a crew of perhaps ten who ride at a crazy tilt atop hiking boards when the boats sail to weather.

Racing of log canoes is said to have started in St. Michaels as early as 1859.

Mustang, a five-log sailing canoe hull with cruising
accommodations added, was for years berthed
along the city docks in Annapolis for day charters.
Built in 1907, the 60-foot *Mustang* recently
was donated to the Chesapeake Bay Maritime
Museum.

Under puffy clouds, smooth water and just the
right amount of wind give *Persistence* a beautiful
upwind sail on the Chester River. The crew hikes
out on planks over the windward side to keep the
boat balanced against its enormous sail area.

Billie P. Hall, originally built in 1903, was in daily use as a motorized workboat at the time she was purchased for racing, but considerable work was necessary before she could be made ready. The engine was removed, extensive work was completed on sails, masts, and the hull, and she became a tough competitor.

An unsuspecting cruiser on the Miles River passes
between *Magic* and *Island Bird*, two long-standing
racing competitors.

OVERLEAF:

Sailing toward the windward mark, *Edmee S.* holds
a steady course with her crew hiked out on the
boards. Owned by the Chesapeake Bay Maritime
Museum in St. Michaels, *Edmee S.* was restored
for racing in 1980.

OPPOSITE TOP:

Running downwind is the five-log canoe *Mystery*, recently returned to the Miles River following a two-year refit. *Mystery* was built in Oxford in 1932 by Harry Sinclair and his son.

OPPOSITE BOTTOM:

The crew of *Mystery* takes to the windward side of the sailing canoe in the Miles River. With all its crew as movable ballast—except a mainsheet trimmer in the outrigger seat and a helmsman—*Mystery* holds her course and her balance.

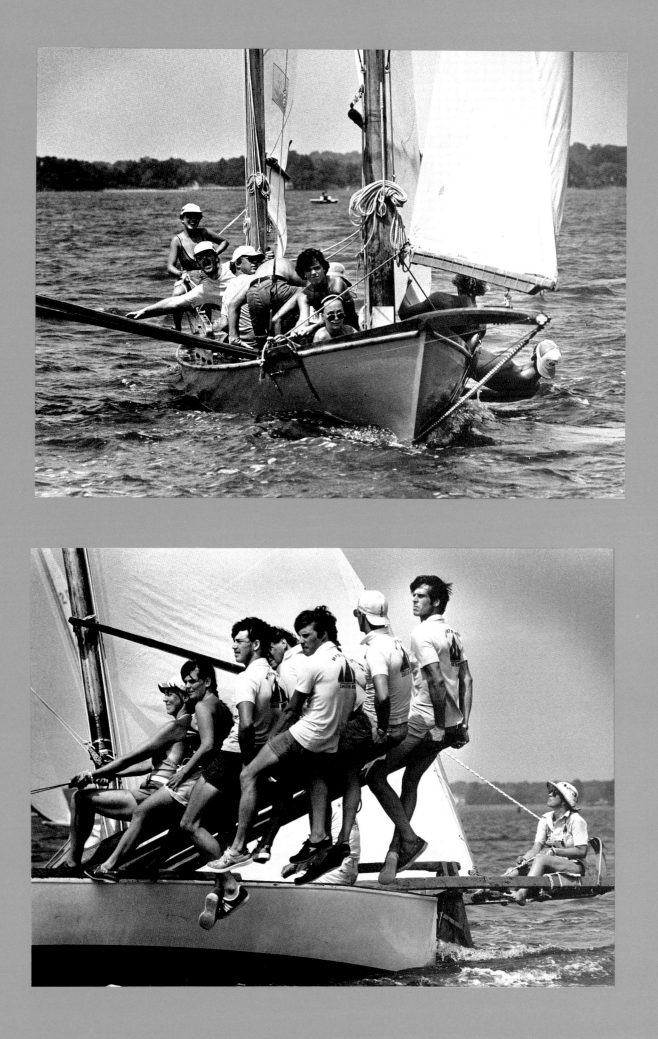

Flying Cloud (right), back on the Chesapeake after a long absence, competes in her first race following renovation. *Mystery* keeps *Flying Cloud* to her weather beam, as the two fight for position on their way to a mark. *Flying Cloud* was built by the late John B. Harrison of Tilghman Island in 1932.

ABOVE:

At the jibe mark during a race, *Noddy* has capsized and her crew works to right her while *S.C. Debson* approaches the mark. *Noddy* was built in 1930 by Oliver Duke of Royal Oak, Maryland. *S.C. Debson*, a three-log canoe, was built in 1895 by James Lowery of Tilghman Island.

OPPOSITE:

Island Bird capsizes in the Miles River as her crew tries valiantly to right her in a freshening breeze. Despite her small size, the *Bird* is a consistent competitor.

OVERLEAF:

Just before the start of the Harris Creek race one season, the helmsman let go of the tiller to take a photograph—and presently *Island Lark* was on her way over. Sails and springboards all were headed toward the water, as in the background *Island Bird* glided toward the starting line.

One of five *Island* canoes built by William Sidney Covington at Tilghman Island, *Island Blossom* is the sister of the legendary *Island Bird*. The *Island Blossom*, 32-feet, 6-inches on deck, was built in 1892. At the time this photograph was taken, *Blossom* was owned by Judge John C. North of Easton, whose family owns and races three log canoes each year. In the photo, *Blossom*'s crew leaps to the hiking boards to keep her upright in a race on the Miles River in 1979.

Island Life

As you cruise south from Annapolis on Chesapeake Bay, the Western Shore stands largely solid and formidable down to the mouth of the Patuxent River, beyond to the Potomac, and down past the rivers Rappahannock, York, and James.

The Eastern Shore is a more complicated matter, a shoreline broken by the mouths of large bays and crooked rivers, each shaped into thousands of snug anchorages and harbors by hooks and necks of solid land or spits of sand and swatches or broads of marsh.

Where the land is hard and fast—from the Bay Bridges to the Little Choptank River—it is a shoreline under attack, as developers battle to build tracts of waterfront housing and condominiums on parcels that for centuries have been barren shores.

Below the Little Choptank, where the hard land begins to fade fast away through the Big Broads and Barren Island Gap, across Tar Bay to the Hooper Islands and beyond, nature mostly reclaims the shore.

From the flats of the Honga River down through Hooper Strait and into Tangier Sound—past Bishops Head Marsh, Dames Quarter and Chance, past Pungers Cove, Muscle Hole, Jericho Marsh, Sheep Pen Gut, and Terrapin Sand— much of the water is thin, and the land, at times, is swept away by wind, wave, and flood tides.

But the watermen and islanders, those who make their livelihood among the same forces that threaten them, remain.

OPPOSITE TOP:

Looking out across the town docks at Ewell on Smith Island, oyster and crab boats lie still in their berths as day nears an end. Smith Island, 75 miles southeast of Washington, D.C., is separated from the Eastern Shore mainland by Tangier Sound and is accessible only by boat.

OPPOSITE BOTTOM:

Seagull, a skipjack loaded with its catch from a hard January day, pushes through an open channel in the ice at Knapps Narrows on Tilghman Island. Not all winters are as harsh, but in the late 1970s and early 1980s, there was much ice on the Bay.

OVERLEAF:

Seagull returns after a cold day of dredging for oysters. A push boat—a small, motorized boat that is raised and lowered from the skipjack's stern to assist in tight maneuvers or to get the larger boat home when the wind dies—propels the skipjack through a channel in the ice.

Oyster boats rest in the ice-filled water of Knapps Narrows at Tilghman Island. Despite ice on the rivers and creeks of the Bay, watermen still went out that day to catch their limit.

A.J. Coleman of Kent Island uses a swab to sweep the snow from the decks of his 36-foot oyster boat docked in the commercial basin at Kent Narrows.

OPPOSITE:

Jesse Brimer of Smith Island checks his slough boxes, entrapments that hold "peeler" crabs until they shed their shells and become soft crabs. Once the crabs are soft, they become great delicacies—and soon are on their way to crab houses up and down the East Coast. The Smith Island–Crisfield area of Maryland is the center of the soft crab industry.

ABOVE:

A resident of Ewell on Smith Island surveys a crab skiff left in the shallows over the winter. As spring nears, the skiff will receive a new coat of paint and some caulk—and soon it will be time to go crabbing.

OVERLEAF:

A pair of shipwrights repair the stem of *Virginia Wade* as she sits on blocks at Severn Marine Services at Knapps Narrows on Tilghman Island.

Slough boxes beside a makeshift walkway line the
marsh grass areas around Ewell harbor. Crabbers
place the boxes in the water and fill them with
crabs that are about to lose their shells. Shedding
is necessary so that crabs, which have no internal
skeletons, can increase in size.

Looking across the marshland at the end of
Rhodes Point on Smith Island, a faithful mate
awaits the return of a captain. *Maxine* is used for
oystering in the winter and crabbing through the
rest of the year.

OVERLEAF:
Stored in the marsh grass at Ewell on Smith
Island, a crab skiff and slough boxes await spring,
a fresh coat of paint, and soft-shelled crabs.

A Labrador retriever makes an interesting hood ornament for a car being driven from Ewell to Rhodes Point on the only road of any size on Smith Island.

The *Island Belle* once ferried mail, provisions, and passengers across Tangier Sound from Crisfield to Smith Island. Now, tied along a shoreline of oyster shells, she serves only as a link to the past.

An old-timer on Smith Island, Emory Evans, loads crab pots atop his car for the trip to his boat. Evans will take the pots, each of which is baited, weighted, and strung to a buoy, into Tangier Sound and set them overboard. Evans will check the crab traps every few days.

After a day on the water, a group gathers in the
late afternoon sun outside the Tylerton general
store to discuss the day's events. The topics might
range from A to Z—but mostly the talk is of
crabs and oysters.

Frances Kitching's home on Smith Island was a bed-and-breakfast inn long before anyone used the term. Tourists have been riding the ferry from Crisfield for years to get a taste of Mrs. Kitching's sautéed soft-shell crabs, clam puffs, pan-browned wild duck, oyster puffs, pies, and cakes.

OPPOSITE TOP:

It is a private world that Paul Marshall carves—
a swampland of marine animals, birds, ducks,
and geese—a place well-suited to the colors of
a master's hand and a waterman's memory.

OPPOSITE BOTTOM:

Woodcarver Paul Marshall of Tylerton stands in
his studio with a piece of his artwork. As a young
man he crabbed on the bay; later, he opened his
own crab house on Smith Island, buying and
shipping soft crabs to large eastern markets.
Marshall's years on the Bay have given his carving
a realism that others may lack.

OVERLEAF:

A pair of rowing prams have sunk beneath the bow
of a workboat in the still waters of Kent Cove.

The setting sun casts shadows on serene Kent
Cove, where prams and skiffs rest quietly at their
pilings. The boats in the foreground are used
primarily to ferry watermen to their workboats,
which are moored farther offshore. In recent
years, the serenity of Kent Cove has been
shattered by the construction of condos and tracts
of housing.

A skiff, partially filled with water from a recent
thunderstorm, is tied off on shore. Left in the
boat are some of the tools of the crabber's
trade. Offshore, the heavyweights of the crabbing
industry are moored.

Come the start of the Maryland crab season, on April 1, these markers piled up at Ewell on Smith Island will be attached to pots and set across the tidal rifts in Tangier Sound.

Under Sail and Power

From the celebrated boats built in the yards of Deltaville, Virginia, to the yachts and workboats that sprang from Jim Richardson's small marine railway along LeCompte Creek off the Choptank River, to the *Prides of Baltimore* built by Peter Boudreau along that city's Inner Harbor, the Chesapeake retains a strong maritime heritage.

It is a heritage built on the pit saw, the hammer, and the timeless arc of the adze cutting into oak and the heartwood of loblolly pine.

It is a heritage that has grown from log sailing canoes to modern racing sloops, from deadrise workboats to plush cabin cruisers—from the beginnings at Jamestown and St. Mary's City to the sprawl of the Washington–Baltimore–Annapolis metroplex and Norfolk–Newport News.

And on almost any day from mid-March to late November, a mix of that heritage might easily be found off the mouth of almost any river in the estuary.

The *Pride of Baltimore II* might be found sailing past a line of ocean-going ships waiting to load or unload at the piers in Baltimore; a bugeye converted to pleasure use might be found within hailing distance of a dredging fleet of skipjacks.

Off Annapolis in autumn, *Dove,* a replica of the seventeenth-century ship that first brought settlers to the St. Mary's River, might be found sailing through a modern racing fleet.

For eight or more months of the year, the Chesapeake will open its cruising grounds to gunkholers, its open waters to hundreds of racing fleets, its fishing grounds to the chase of crabs, seatrout, bluefish, spot, and drum.

But then, somewhere between mid-October and late November, the wind will play in and out of the northwest over several days, then steady northwest and blow hard and cold—and the season will be done.

LEFT:

The *Pride of Baltimore*, 86-feet long on deck and with twin, 95-foot masts, was launched at Baltimore's Inner Harbor on February 27, 1977. Constructed of wood and in the manner of the nineteenth-century schooners known as Baltimore Clippers, the *Pride* was based on an 1812 design by Thomas Kemp. On May 14, 1986, a ferocious storm capsized *Pride* 240 miles from Puerto Rico. The ship's captain and three crew members were drowned. The boat was returning from a goodwill tour to Europe. Two and a half years later, the *Pride of Baltimore II* was launched, with several improvements in equipment and design.

BELOW:

A young crew member of the Norwegian sail-training ship *Christian Radich* looks aft from the bowsprit as the vessel powers down the Potomac River from Washington D.C. in April, 1976.

ABOVE:

Dove enjoys a good breeze to fill her sails.

OPPOSITE:

Dove, a replica of the small ship that brought the first settlers to Maryland's St. Mary's River in 1634, reaches along north of the Bay Bridges during a visit to the annual Chesapeake Appreciation Days festival at Sandy Point State Park between Annapolis and Baltimore. *Dove* and a replica of a companion ship, *Ark*, usually are berthed at St. Mary's City, where they are open to visitors.

ABOVE:

Reaching along, *J.N. Carter*, a square-stern bugeye built in Massachusetts, works her way north on the Chesapeake. Built as a pleasure craft, the boat also was used to carry freight and once hauled a load of watermelons to Baltimore.

OPPOSITE:

Members of the Chesapeake Bristol Club raft together at Gray's Inn Creek off the Chester River. The club sponsors about a dozen such gatherings each season. Some members race to the rendezvous from Annapolis and others cruise from their respective berths around the Bay.

OVERLEAF:

The 34-foot C&C design *Speculation* takes a knockdown after setting her spinnaker during the annual fall race series south of the Bay Bridges.

OPPOSITE:

The Cal 29 *Uh–Oh* races before a storm along the Severn River.

OVERLEAF:

A few boats managed to strip to bare poles before a squall struck near Annapolis harbor, but there was trouble aboard the Yankee 30 *Repulse II*. Although *Repulse II* rode out the squall after a few worried moments, the 50-knot winds were far too much for a small one-design boat that capsized.

OPPOSITE:

With spinnaker newly set, the race boat *Goldfish* chases clouds down the Bay during a spring regatta.

BELOW:

The Chesapeake Bay and its rivers and creeks, with hundreds of coves to anchor in and thousands of miles of shoreline, are prime cruising grounds. Here, a cat boat motors up Glebe Creek, a quiet anchorage on the South River.

For many years, the midshipmen of the United States Naval Academy have left their classrooms to learn a few lessons on the Chesapeake Bay off Annapolis. Here, *Swift*, a 44-foot Luders yawl, takes a knockdown after carrying its spinnaker too far abeam.

Wednesday night racing off Annapolis couldn't have been much worse for this yachtsman as his boom broke at the vang and his spinnaker blew away to port.

OVERLEAF:

At times, spinnakers can be the bane of racing sailors—as some of these Class A boats find out at the start of a long-distance race down Chesapeake Bay.

The 52-foot auxiliary yawl *Karin* trims her sails before a setting sun as she beats out the Delaware River. Forty-eight hours and twenty-two minutes later, she dropped anchor at Great Salt Pond on Block Island, Rhode Island.

Duncan Spencer's 52-foot *Karin* beats to
windward as she leaves Chesapeake Bay and heads
into the Atlantic Ocean. *Karin* was designed by
Henry Gruber and built at the Burmester yacht
yard in Bremen, Germany, in 1951.

OPPOSITE:

Raider, a New York 32, leads a racing fleet out the West River during a Wednesday night race. The West River Sailing Club runs weekly races out of Galesville, Maryland.

The International Offshore Rule racing sloop *Pirana* heads into a roll after popping its spinnaker.

OVERLEAF:

The battle to tame *Pirana's* powerful, tri-radial spinnaker continued for several minutes—despite the best efforts of scrambling crew and a straining helmsman—but the aluminum sloop was laid on its beam ends.

OPPOSITE TOP:

Midshipmen in the training sloop *Bee–Bee* take a reef in the mainsail on a windy day off Annapolis. *Bee–Bee* is in close pursuit of another Academy vessel, *Avenger*.

OPPOSITE BOTTOM:

With the Bay Bridges as a backdrop, an Alberg 30, a popular racer/cruiser, buries its leeward rail.

OVERLEAF:

As the sun sets near Sandy Point, the annual Great Ocean Race gets under way. The race, which circumnavigates the Delmarva peninsula clockwise, usually is held in late May or early June.

The 72-foot yawl *Cotton Blossom* from
Marblehead, Massachusetts, "hardens up" as she
slices through the Bay north of the Bay Bridges.
Cotton Blossom was built in Fairlie, Scotland,
in 1926.

Bob Dull of Annapolis knows both the joy and the
hardship of a good breeze and a fast ride in a 505
one-design sailboat on the Severn River.

OVERLEAF:
Beneath puffy clouds, boats drift in light air with
their spinnakers up and awaiting a freshening
breeze.

OPPOSITE TOP:

Sailing is a daily routine for the midshipmen of the
United States Naval Academy during spring and
fall. In either season, a sudden squall can make
getting back to harbor somewhat difficult.

OPPOSITE TOP:

Caught in a summer downpour, the small English cruising sloop, *Patience*, sails north of the Chesapeake Bay.

OVERLEAF:

A wind-surfer catches a stiff breeze to ride the breaking surf at the entrance to the Chesapeake Bay near Norfolk, Virginia.

Jeanne VI, under full power, moves across the Bay
from St. Michaels on the Eastern Shore to
Galesville on the West River.

A lapstrake express cruiser powers out of the
Severn River through a good chop.

OVERLEAF:

The sportfisherman *Helen B* heads home after a
weekend of fishing on the Bay.

Lois and Jim Duffy enjoy a quiet anchorage for dinner aboard their classic 1956 Century *Raven* near Round Bay on the Severn River above Annapolis.

OPPOSITE:

As thunderheads build quickly in the northeast, a small motor launch heads for shelter in Oxford, Maryland.

OVERLEAF:

Rainy days don't dampen the fun for *Purely Pleasure,* a custom-built offshore power yacht whose twin diesels can move her along at 50 knots.

A classic motor yacht built at the now defunct Trumpy Yacht Yard in Annapolis steams home before a storm. Trumpys, as they are known, are highly prized for their elegant designs and fine workmanship.

OVERLEAF:

Long and narrow, 990 feet by 101 feet 6 inches, and with four engines, the S.S. *United States* once held the record for fastest Atlantic passage—3 days, 10 hours and 40 minutes, at an average of 35.59 knots. The S.S. *United States* started its run on July 3, 1952, establishing a record that stood for more than 30 years.

On the bridge of the S.S. *United States*, as she sat in Norfolk harbor in 1980, a life ring is draped over one of her wheels, abandoned the day she stopped service in 1969. The ship now lies at Newport News, Virginia.

OVERLEAF:

A lifeboat breaks through heavy seas to carry provisions to an international cargo ship anchored off Annapolis and awaiting its turn at the coal pier in Baltimore.

Acknowledgments

My work on this book was greatly aided by many people and institutions:

My wife Georgia's warm company during those long, cold days driving the back roads of the Eastern Shore, bouncing across wave tops, and carrying my heavy camera bag made this project a happy experience; her organizational skills and words of encouragement also helped enormously.

My deepest thanks go to Peter Baker for his ability to create pictures with words, and to Craig Biggs for all those days at the helm of *Kodachrome*, braving the elements to put me in position to make my pictures.

Memories of time spent cruising the South River, and that first wild and crazy sail aboard a log canoe with John Chamberlin come alive for me again. I thank Marion (Junior) and Bobbie Marshall for making me a part of their lives and a part of the Eastern Shore.

James A. Michener's advice and encouragement while walking through the pine grove along Broad Creek were a tremendous influence in my work.

I was fortunate to have had special support from Betty Rigoli, always the "Chief," and forever willing to take a chance on my projects and lend a helping hand; and from Ed Dunaway, who gave me the down payment for my first photo boat.

Richard Royer's professional assistance and positive vision throughout the years have made a great contribution to this book.

Those wonderful sailing adventures with Duncan Spencer are warmly remembered here. John Sherwood is a friend never forgotten for having taught me how to sail.

My family have been of immeasurable help. My sister Mary's words of encouragement endure forever. With great affection I thank my brother William for those times he drove my boat as we were knocked off our feet by the force of the seas and soaked from the spray of waves. And for all her support I salute my mom.

I am also thankful for the various help received from: Jim Bailey, Clarence Blackwell, William E. Boone, Bernie Boston, John Bowden, Calvert Marine Museum, Gloria Chamberlin, Members of the Chesapeake Bay Log Canoe Association, *Chesapeake Bay Magazine*, Chesapeake Bay Maritime Museum, Tom Curley, Tom Dardin, Christopher and Kathleen Davis, Bob and Alverta Dietz, Jim and Lois Duffy, David Dunigan, Carl Griebel, Lee Griebel, Bill and Faith Hanlon, Ken Heinen, Bob Herman, Bobby Huntington, Micca Hutchins, Clarence "Renny" Johnson, Michael C. Kumer, "Pepper" Langley, Stanley Larrimore, Glen Leach, Ray Lustig, Mariner's Museum, Bob Marshall, Howard Merrideth, Miles River Yacht Club, and Pat Patterson (Topaz Yachts).

Bob Grieser